PROPHETIC PREACHING

THE MISSING JEWEL OF THE EVANGELICAL CHURCH?

WALLACE BENN

The Latimer Trust

Scripture quotations are taken from the English Standard Version (ESV) The Holy Bible, English Standard Version. ESV® Text Edition: 2016. Copyright © 2001 by Crossway Bibles, a publishing ministry of Good News Publishers.

New International Version (NIV) Holy Bible, New International Version®, NIV® Copyright ©1973, 1978, 1984, 2011 by Biblica, Inc.® Used by permission. All rights reserved worldwide.

The Latimer Trust (formerly Latimer House, Oxford) is a conservative Evangelical research organisation within the Church of England, whose main aim is to promote the history and theology of Anglicanism as understood by those in the Reformed tradition. Interested readers are welcome to consult its website for further details of its many activities.

The Latimer Trust
London N14 4PS UK
Registered Charity: 1084337
Company Number: 4104465
Web: www.latimertrust.org
E-mail: administrator@latimertrust.org

Contents

Foreword

I am delighted that Wallace has written in such an informed way on the relationship between preaching and prophecy, and therefore the significance of proclamation and application.

Preaching as I was growing up was certainly biblical, if pietistic, but quite frequently the text was a 'launching pad' into other parts of Scripture. However, such a sermon was often warm in application: it was a 'message'. More recently, conservative evangelicals have thankfully rediscovered the centrality of true expository preaching, often from a longer (sometimes too long?) passage of God's Word. We can rightly be thankful for the outstanding ministries of men like Martyn Lloyd-Jones, David Jackman, Dick Lucas, and John Stott. But we can be very weak on application because we have not grasped the reality of the prophetic element, and so preaching has sometimes concluded, if lengthily, high and dry.

Wallace's careful writing will redress the balance, and it is much needed.

Tony Baker

'It is this sense of the word from God – this great idea of prophesying – which brings us a little nearer, perhaps, to understanding preaching'.

D.M. Lloyd-Jones, 'What is Preaching?' in *Knowing the Times* (Edinburgh: Banner of Truth, 1989), p. 276.

Many evangelical churches which are not convinced about the cessationist argument that the miraculous gifts of the Holy Spirit ended with the Apostles ask themselves about how to practically exercise prophetic ministry in the local congregation today. Paul tells us that this ministry is one we should seek, that it is very valuable and that it brings 'upbuilding and encouragement and consolation' to people (1 Cor 14:1, 3). Some of the attempts at this practice in churches have caused both division and concern, and have sometimes distracted from the belief in both the sufficiency of Holy Scripture and the priority of expository preaching as the key ingredients in the life of a healthy church.

Local church expectation has not been helped by the practice at some large Christian events. I remember one such event where we heard an excellent and moving exposition of Isaiah 53. After the preacher had finished, the platform leader said; 'That was great, but let's now have time for the "now Word of the Lord"'! The implication was clear, the 'prophetic' ministry to follow was more exciting and relevant to our lives today. This is just bad practice and a complete misunderstanding of the fact that what the Holy Spirit said in Scripture, he still says today (see Hebrews 3:7). The Bible is the 'now Word of the Lord' for us!

Introductory issues

In helping us to steer a safe course through some of the complexity of the arguments about prophecy in the New

Testament, Wayne Grudem's *The Gift of Prophecy* has been very influential and persuasive to a lot of people.[1] Grudem argues that unlike Old Testament prophecy, New Testament prophecy is fallible. Errors may occur because what God prompted in the first place is fallibly communicated by the prophet. So, in New Testament prophecy it is inappropriate to use words like 'Thus said the Lord' as one of the canonical prophets of the Old Testament would have been accurate and comfortable in saying. Grudem's work has thankfully put a brake on excessive claims for prophecy today that can and do undermine the supreme authority of Holy Scripture. He is scrupulously clear and right in affirming that the New Testament Apostles are the equivalent of Old Testament canonical prophets, and that their teaching is always paramount.

However, Grudem's thesis is not above criticism. Don Carson, in a sympathetic review that accepts the main drift of Grudem's view, warns of two dangers.[2]

1. 'First, the thesis oversimplifies the contrast between Old Testament prophets, and New Testament prophets. The Old Testament, for instance, records the existence of "schools" of the prophets; and it is far from clear that everyone in

---

[1] Wayne Grudem, *The Gift of Prophecy in the New Testament and Today* (Eastbourne: Kingsway, 1988).

[2] D. A. Carson, *Showing the Spirit* (Grand Rapids: Baker, 1987), 98–99.

a particular "school" enjoyed the status of Amos or Isaiah'.

2. 'Secondly, Grudem describes the two levels of authority as, respectively, an authority of general content and an authority that extends to the very words of the prophet. This goes beyond the evidence and is open to several objections... What evidence is there that it was a different gift, so far as the prophet's self-perceptions were concerned?'

3. However, he concludes, having made the necessary qualifications, that, 'It will not do to question his entire thesis because we have questions about some of his formulations.'

The more recent criticisms of Grudem's views by Thomas Schreiner are a good deal more trenchant and telling.[3] They are as follows:

1. 'First, the judging of prophecies does not indicate that prophets could err [contra Grudem], for in the Old Testament the only way to determine whether someone was a true prophet was by assessing prophecies. If the prophecies were mistaken, the person was not a true prophet. (See Deut 18:21–22; 1 Sam 3:19–20)'.

---

[3] Thomas R. Schreiner, *1 Corinthians*, Tyndale NT Commentaries (Downers Grove, IL: IVP, 2018), 260f.

2. 'Second, Agabus was not mistaken in Acts 21:11 [Grudem claims he got details wrong], since when Paul recounts the story of his arrest in Acts 28:17, he appeals to the very word Agabus used [Gk: paradidomi] to describe Paul being handed over to the Romans. We have further evidence that Agabus spoke as a prophet of the Lord ... the words of Agabus reflect a prophetic formula, "The Holy Spirit says" (Acts 21:11).'

3. 'Third, in Acts 21:4 the prophecy was Spirit-inspired and accurate (Paul would suffer), but the inference drawn from the prophecy (Paul should not go to Jerusalem) is mistaken.'

In summing up Schreiner says the following:

> I conclude that the prophetic gift in the New Testament is of the same nature as the gift in the Old Testament. God communicates, typically spontaneously, revelations by his prophets which are authoritative and completely true.[4]

Therefore, Schreiner does not believe the gift of prophecy continues today (in its canonical sense), as the period of New Testament revelation has ended. But further, agreeing with Carson, he says, 'Thus, prophecy could be

---

[4] Schreiner, *1 Corinthians*, 261

granted during preaching since it provides insight into what a person (or group) needs to hear.'[5]

In Wayne Grudem's latest edition of his magnum opus, *Systematic Theology*, he restates his position with some further clarifications and engages with Schreiner and others who have been unconvinced by his basic thesis.[6] Many of Grudem's views are interesting and his cautions are extremely helpful. Let me mention some of them:

1. 'So, prophecy has less authority than "teaching", and prophecies in the church are always to be subject to the authoritative teaching of Scripture' (p. 310).

2. 'The task of interpreting and applying Scripture, then, is called "teaching" in the New Testament'. (p. 1310) However, in my view, this very much needs qualification.

3. 'People who continually seek subjective "messages" from God to guide their lives must be cautioned that subjective personal guidance is not a primary function of New Testament prophecy. They need to place much more emphasis on Scripture and seeking God's sure wisdom written there' (p. 1311).

---

[5] Schreiner, *1 Corinthians*, 259.
[6] Wayne Grudem, *Systematic Theology: An Introduction To Biblical Doctrine* (Nottingham: IVP, 2020), 1293–1313.

4. 'If the gift of prophecy begins to be used in a church, the church should place even more emphasis on the vastly superior value of Scripture as the source to which Christians can always go to hear the voice of the living God. Prophecy is a valuable gift, as are many other gifts, but it is in Scripture that God and only God speaks to us his very words, even today, and throughout our lives' (p. 1313).

5. 'And rather than seeking guidance through prophecy, we should emphasise that it is in Scripture that we are to find guidance for our lives (p. 1313).

We are indebted to Grudem for these sensible Scripture-honouring cautions, which need to be taken to heart in the life of every evangelical congregation contemplating these matters.

What then are the difficulties with his view?

As we shall see, prophecy is a wide category word and by narrowing it down to spontaneous 'impressions' or 'promptings' which are fallible he unintentionally misleads us.

The key to a better understanding is three things, I believe:

1. To see that not just fresh revelation, but faithful exposition of what Moses revealed, with

application to the present needs of the people enabled by the Holy Spirit, was called prophecy by the later 'minor' prophets.

2. Peter shows us in Acts 2 all the helpful ingredients of this kind of authentic prophetic preaching. His preaching was the product of prayerfulness and deep reflection on Holy Scripture and the teaching of Jesus in the light of the Easter event. He displays Spirit-enabled exposition and proclamation of the gospel, which calls for a response to the risen Lord Jesus Christ, who is the Saviour of all who turn to him in repentance and faith.

3. It is important to note the following comments: 'The interpretation of Scripture, usually in the synagogues, is a central feature of the mission of the prophets, though it is not confined to them' and 'the role of the prophet may overlap that of the elder as it does that of the apostle and teacher, especially in certain teaching functions'.[7]

Paul writes to the Corinthians: 'Pursue love, and earnestly desire the spiritual gifts, especially that you may prophesy' (1 Cor 14:1). It is surely this kind of expository gospel preaching with application, which is Spirit-enabled and prompted, that the church most needs today. Peter

---

[7] Colin Brown, evaluating the work of E. E. Ellis on the subject in *The New International Dictionary of New Testament Theology* (Exeter: Paternoster, 1986), 8/f.

models it for us in his sermon in Acts 2. This is what brings 'upbuilding and encouragement and consolation' (1 Cor 14:3). It is this kind of preaching that, as on the day of Pentecost, brings conviction of God's presence to an unbeliever and reveals the secrets of his heart (in other words, that he is a sinner and needs a Saviour) (1 Cor 14:24–25).

It is the gospel that does that as 'the power of God unto salvation', not some 'clairvoyant' type of revelation about some secondary detail in a person's life. Calvin warns that it is unthinkable to contemplate the church without this kind of prophetic gift, whereas the 'promptings' as Grudem describes them, though valuable in their place, would surely not have been given the elevated status that Paul gives to prophecy here!

As I am not a strict cessationist, I have no problem with accepting that one aspect of prophecy may be the Holy Spirit's helpful prompting of a person or church in a particular direction at a needy moment which, as it is localised, does not need to be enscripturated or elevated to Scriptural status. But surely now that the Son has revealed the Father's will for the salvation of a world-wide people redeemed by his grace for his glory, there is no need for further revelations other than given to us by Holy Scripture. It is not only authoritative but 'sufficient' for all the essential needs of God's people.

In these 'last days' the prophetic preaching of the Word of God already revealed in the Holy Scriptures must surely

It is surely this kind of expository gospel preaching with application, which is Spirit-enabled and prompted, that the church most needs today.

be the main ingredient of a healthy and fruitful church life. Prayerful, Spirit-enabled teaching, that is preached with careful application that calls for a response is our primary need – not to look for excitement elsewhere! It is that which we should earnestly seek and ask God for, above all other gifts, while acknowledging that prophecy can, on occasions, cover other phenomena at a local church level. However, New Testament prophecy is always 'testimony to Jesus' and is essentially expository. This fits with my observation and experience of so called 'prophecy' today, which has largely been – though not always – a pointing out with application to present needs of what Scripture already teaches.

A word needs to be said about Grudem's understanding of Ephesians 2:20, 'built on the foundation of the apostles and prophets'. He takes the phrase to mean 'apostles who are also prophets'. While possible, this has not had general consent among good commentators, and Grudem now acknowledges that it is not central to his argument. Clearly, as Hodge and most modern commentators state, this refers to New Testament prophets as Ephesians 3:5 and 4:11 make clear. But the prophets in 2:20 are best understood, with John Stott, as a group around the Apostles supporting and proclaiming the same apostolic message about God's plan of redemption in Christ:

> The reference must again be to a small group of inspired teachers, associated with the apostles, who together bore witness to Christ and whose teaching

was derived from revelation (Eph. 3:5) and was foundational. In practical terms this means that the church is built on the New Testament Scriptures.[8]

With the Apostles they laid the foundation that the church in every age is dependent upon. The prophets in the Corinthian church are not necessarily the same people!

Alec Motyer's comments are very helpful:

> Prophecy in 1 Corinthians 14:29–33 would seem to be not prediction but the declaration of some truth from and of God – as seen to be the case in 1 Thessalonians 5:20. Throughout 1 Corinthians 14, Paul's desire is that, in whatever way God shall choose, the gathered assembly should be edified by the intelligible truth (verses 4–5, 11, 17, 19). In this, the prophets have their part, as we suggested above, bringing the truth about Jesus to light in the context of the Scriptures they possessed.

Furthermore, commenting on Ephesians 2:20, he explains:

> Paul may be referring to Apostles as the foundational agents of revelation and the

[8] John R. W. Stott, *The Message of Ephesians: God's New Society*, BST (Leicester: IVP, 1979), 107.

prophets as those gifted by God within local churches to bring out and apply scriptural truth in the light of Christ.[9]

F. F. Bruce also helpfully comments:

> The church is built upon the twofold foundation of apostles and prophets ... the apostles representing the authority of primary witness to the gospel facts, while the prophets represent the living guidance of the Spirit by which the facts were apprehended in ever fuller meaning and scope.[10]

Prophecy in the New Testament, as modelled in Acts 2

I am, however, getting ahead of myself! The purpose of this paper is to ask us to look again at the main ingredients of prophecy in the New Testament.

Prophecy is a wide-ranging term and covers a lot of different things: 'prophecy may denote a gift or activity as broad and general as declaring or telling forth the revealed will of God'.[11] It can cover praise in music

---

9 Alec Motyer and Steve Motyer, *Discovering 1 & 2 Thessalonians*, Crossway Bible Guides (Leicester: Crossway, 1999), 113–114.

10 F. F. Bruce, 'Ephesians' in *New International Commentary on the New Testament* (Grand Rapids: Eerdmans, 1988), 315.

11 Anthony C. Thiselton, *1 Corinthians: A Shorter Exegetical and Pastoral Commentary* (Grand Rapids: Eerdmans, 2006), 201.

as well as foretelling and forthtelling (2 Chron 15:3). However, my desire is to enable us to see, with the help of Peter's sermon in Acts 2, what are the fundamental ingredients of prophetic ministry. I am not attempting to give a comprehensive 'catch all' kind of definition but to get to the heart of the issue. Nor am I trying to give a full elaboration of all that could be said about prophecy in the New Testament. Rather I want to show you the central elements to prophecy which are displayed so well in Peter's preaching on the Day of Pentecost.

Bearing witness to Jesus

The book of Revelation tells us that the spirit of prophecy is the testimony of Jesus: 'I am a fellow servant with you and with your brothers and sisters who hold to the testimony of Jesus. Worship God! For it is the Spirit of prophecy who bears testimony to Jesus'. (Rev 19:10, NIV). Regarding the last phrase, G. K. Beale helpfully says that its meaning is: 'those giving testimony to Jesus are prophetic people'.[12] That is a central truth. Every aspect of prophetic ministry that is genuine will bear witness to and seek to glorify the Lord Jesus Christ, and not distract us from worshipping him. So, our personal testimony to God's gracious saving and keeping work in our lives is prophetic.

---

[12] G. K. Beale, *Revelation: A Shorter Commentary* (Grand Rapids: Eerdmans, 2015), 407.

In the crucial passage from Joel that Peter uses to explain the phenomena on the Day of Pentecost, God promised that there would come a day when:

> I will pour out my Spirit on all flesh, and your sons and your daughters shall prophesy, and your young men shall see visions, and your old men shall dream dreams; even on my male servants and female servants in those days I will pour out my Spirit, and they shall prophesy (Acts 2:17–18, Joel 2:28–29).

This has now happened, says Peter (Acts 2:15-16). The speaking in tongues or languages so that everyone has an opportunity to hear the gospel in their own tongue is a marker showing the beginning of the fulfilment of Joel's prophecy that all God's people will prophesy. Christians are all called to testify to Jesus and to what God has done to save a people for his own possession through the life, death and resurrection of the Lord Jesus.

I very much like the comment of Raymond Dillard:

> Protestant theology is accustomed to speaking of the 'priesthood of all believers'; perhaps in light of Acts 2 and Joel 2:28–32, we must also speak of the 'prophethood of all believers' ... all who call on the name of the Lord (2:32) now have the equipage and the obligation

> incumbent upon prophets to bear witness
> to their generation.[13]

Being witnesses to our Lord and Saviour is no optional extra in the Christian life, but part and parcel of what we are meant to be and do. The risen Jesus had promised the disciples, 'You will receive power when the Holy Spirit has come upon you, and you will be my witnesses in Jerusalem and in all Judea and Samaria, and to the end of the earth' (Acts 1:8).

If speaking the gospel in different languages to different people heralded the universal reach of the good news, it was also prophetic testimony to the risen Christ and his on-going ministry. It was the fulfilment of Joel's prophecy. That is widely understood. What is less well noticed is that Peter's sermon on the day explaining what had happened and what it testified to about Jesus and the gospel was also prophecy – it was prophetic preaching.

David Peterson helpfully comments: 'Peter's extensive and carefully argued speech has a prophetic character and is as much a Spirit-inspired utterance as the speaking in other languages'.[14] Peter's concern is to convince the crowd that Jesus is the promised Messiah, and that God had already attested to who he is by 'mighty works and wonders and signs' during his earthly ministry, that his

---

[13] Thomas Edward McComiskey, ed., 'Joel', in *The Minor Prophets* (Grand Rapids: Baker, 1992), 295.

[14] David G. Peterson, *The Acts of the Apostles* (Grand Rapids: Eerdmans/Apollos, 2009), 139.

crucifixion was all part of God's plan, and that because of who he is and what he did God raised him from the dead (Acts 2:22–24). Peter concluded his sermon with these words: 'Let all the house of Israel therefore know for certain that God has made him both Lord and Christ, this Jesus whom you crucified' (Acts 2:36). In a special and particular way, through his Spirit-inspired and enabled preaching, Peter is testifying to who the Lord Jesus is and what he has done for us.

To quote David Peterson again:

> However, in Acts, the knowledge of God which the Spirit kindles in believers comes from the glorified Christ through the preaching of the gospel. This knowledge of God then becomes the basis of ministry to others through the gospel and the operation of the Spirit ... 'Prophesying' appears to be a particular way of describing Spirit-directed ministry, both to believers and unbelievers.[15]

So, any testimony to our Saviour whether in the ordinary believer's witness or in the particular gift of Christ-exalting preaching of the gospel has the essential nature of prophecy for it is Spirit-dependent and Spirit-enabled (John 15:26–27). Prophecy ranges from personal testimony generally, to the specific calling of gospel preaching and exposition.

---

[15] Peterson, *Acts*, 142.

Expounding the Scriptures

I love the comment I heard R. T. Kendall make, that 'the church was born in expository preaching'. When you analyse Peter's sermon in Acts 2, it is clear that the structure is built around the carefully considered exposition of three passages from Holy Scripture – Joel 2, Psalm 16 and Psalm 110 – how they were fulfilled then and there on the Day of Pentecost, and their application to what was happening as the result of the death, resurrection and exaltation of Jesus the Messiah. We will look later at the detail of what Peter teaches and preaches, as an authoritative Apostle of the Lord Jesus who has understood the Old Testament in the light of the instruction of the risen Jesus to him and the rest of the disciples. But for now, notice that his prophetic preaching centred around expounding and explaining God's promises in the Old Testament. The revelation and accomplishment of God's plan of salvation now revealed had been promised long before.

It was my old Principal, mentor and friend, J. Alec Motyer, who alerted me a long time ago to a very important point in relation to prophecy in the New Testament:

> This teaches us that the prophets were not sources of new truth to the church, but expounders of truth otherwise revealed. Just as the OT prophets stood in a subordinate relation to Moses, who provided the doctrinal norm of sound

teaching, so the NT prophet stood towards the Apostles, and was bound to submit all to the test of that which they declared as the word of God.[16]

Calvin agrees:

> I am certain, in my own mind, that he means by prophets, not those endowed with the gift of foretelling, but those who were blessed with the unique gift of dealing with Scripture, not only by interpreting it, but also by the wisdom they showed in making it meet the needs of the hour. From this verse let us therefore learn that prophets are (1) outstanding interpreters of Scripture; and (2) men endowed with extraordinary wisdom and aptitude for grasping what the immediate need of the Church is, and speaking the right word to meet it. That is why they are, so to speak, messengers who bring news of what God wants.[17]

A more recent commentary picks up Calvin's second point above:

---

[16] J. A. Motyer, 'Prophecy, Prophets', in *The New Bible Dictionary*, J. D. Douglas, ed., 1st ed. (London: IVF, 1962), 1045.
[17] John Calvin, *Commentary on 1 Corinthians 12:28–31* (Grand Rapids: Eerdmans, 1979), 271.

The second emphasis, on having a special ability to understand 'the immediate need of the Church' and to speak 'the right word to meet it', thus communicating the divine will, is very similar to our own understanding of the prophetic gift (for which the predicting of future events was a secondary and not essential feature).[18]

Calvin summarises:

In a word my view is that the prophets referred to here are those who are skilful and experienced in making known the will of God, by applying prophecies, threats, promises, and all the teaching of Scripture to the current needs of the Church.[19]

J. I. Packer characteristically sums it up helpfully and well:

The essence of the prophetic ministry was forthtelling God's present word to his people, and this regularly meant application of revealed truth rather than augmentation of it. As Old Testament prophets preached the law and recalled Israel to face God's covenant claim

---

[18] Roy E. Ciampa and Brian S. Rosner, *The First Letter to the Corinthians* (Grand Rapids: Eerdmans/Apollos, 2010), 611.

[19] Calvin, *1 Corinthians 12:28–31*, 271.

on their obedience, with promise of blessing if they complied and cursing if not, so it appears that New Testament prophets preached the gospel and the life of faith for conversion, edification and encouragement ... By parity of reasoning, therefore, any verbal enforcement of biblical teaching as it applies to one's present hearers may properly be called prophecy today, for that in truth is what it is.[20]

Some recent important opinion chimes in with the above: 'Prophecy is thus gospel focused and expository in nature'.[21] Also, of particular interest are the following comments by Anthony Thiselton:

Amos views prophetic speech as synonymous with proclamation or preaching (7:16, 'do not prophesy against Israel', is in synonymous parallelism with 'and stop preaching against the house of Isaac', NIV). The near equivalence between prophecy and 'pastoral preaching' in Paul has been urged [by a

---

[20] J. I. Packer, *Keep in Step with the Spirit* (Leicester: IVP, 1990), 215.

[21] Paul Gardner, *1 Corinthians, Zondervan Exegetical Commentary on the New Testament* (Grand Rapids: Zondervan, 2018), 593.

"The essence of the prophetic ministry was forthtelling God's present word to his people".

number of writers.]... Since Paul explicitly defines the aim of prophetic speech as 'to edify, exhort, and encourage, it coincides therefore to a large extent with what we call a sermon today'.[22]

Prophetic speech 'built up' the church, both by convincing 'outsiders' of the truth of the gospel (1 Cor 14:24–25) and by the nurturing believers' faith. In the Reformation era Zwingli and Bullinger were nearer to the view outlined here than some today. They identified prophetic discourse with scriptural reflection leading to pastoral application and nurture.[23]

Garland quotes Friedrich as defining prophecy as 'The inspired speech of charismatic preachers through whom God's plan of salvation for the world and the community and His will for the life of individual Christians are made known. The prophet knows something of the divine will (1 Cor 13:2)'.[24]

---

[22] Thiselton, *1 Corinthians*, 201–02, quoting J. Héring, *First Epistle*, 127.

[23] Thiselton, *1 Corinthians*, 201–02.

[24] Gerhard Friedrich, 'Prophetes', in *Theological Dictionary of the New Testament*, Gerhard Kittel and Gerhard Friedrich, eds., trans. Geoffrey W. Bromiley, 10 vols. (Grand Rapids: Eerdmans, 1964–1976), 6:848.

Michael Griffiths in his helpful little book *Cinderella's Betrothal Gifts*, really a supplement to his larger excellent book on the doctrine of the church *Cinderella with Amnesia*, makes the helpful following point:

> It may be objected that the result of this analysis is to suggest that prophecy is almost no more than another word for inspired preaching and teaching. *However, as has been pointed out in our treatment of the whole concept of the spectrum of grace, it cannot be denied from the descriptions given earlier that prophecy does overlap very considerably with preaching, teaching and encouragement.* If Scripture itself describes prophecy in this way, then we must be cautious about pressing an understanding of the word which relies more on its English derivation than on Scriptural usage.[25]

Fore-telling

I have already made it clear, I hope, that though prophecy can include the fore-telling of future events, it is not essentially that, but much more about forth-telling of the revealed word of God. That is a surprise to many who think prophecy is all about future prediction.

---

[25] Michael Griffiths, *Cinderella's Betrothal Gifts* (Sevenoaks: OMF Books, 1978), 35 (emphasis added).

Another crucial factor needs to be born in mind: the Apostles testified to the 'mystery revealed', as Paul puts it in Ephesians, that God's plan of salvation to include Jews and Gentiles through the gospel in the church of Jesus Christ has now happened (Eph 3:7–13). The climax of God's saving purposes have been revealed in the coming of the Lord Jesus as the book of Hebrews makes clear. 'In these last days God has spoken to us by his Son' (Hebrews 1:2). We are now living in the last days, and await the return in glory of our Saviour, the Lord Jesus Christ. What we need to know about the present and the future has been revealed in him, and in the pages of the New Testament which contains the inspired apostolic witness of all that God achieved through his Son for our salvation and blessing.

The Book of Revelation spells out to us, in great brush strokes, that in the future the world will see that 'The Lamb wins' – to use the title of a great little book by Richard Bewes. All that every Christian really needs to know about the future is revealed in the pages of Scripture. Revelation ends with a warning about adding to or taking away from the 'words of the book of this prophecy' (Rev 22:18–19). Not everything we would *like* to know about the future, but all we *need* to know to rejoice in Christ about our future hope, has been revealed in the revelation of God in Christ and his glorious gospel. Why do we need to know more? The Holy Scriptures have a back cover, and all that every generation of Christians needs to know for faith and godliness is revealed therein. The Bible is sufficient, as well as being our final authority in all matters of faith and morals, until we see our Saviour face to face!

Application

There is an interesting overlap between preaching and teaching in the ministry of the Lord Jesus (see for example, Luke 4:14–15, 44). What makes preaching distinct from teaching is not the content but rather that it is teaching with exhortation to take seriously and put into practice. The preacher comes from the presence of God, having taken his Word seriously himself, and preaches the same with an urgency and an authority that comes from God himself. This is the kind of arresting preaching that we see in Peter's sermon in Acts 2. It comes across with relevance and application to those who are listening. The power in the preaching comes from the content, it is a message from God, and also the fact that it has touched the preacher's heart, as well as being Spirit-anointed and enabled in its delivery.

It comes across not simply as information but a message from the living God who calls for a response to what he says. It is preaching which not only informs but requires a verdict. It is truth, which speaks into a situation, with application that people can see.

So, I believe, application is very important in preaching. Not a forced application, nor an application thin on biblical support, but rather an application which comes from understanding what the Word of God meant to those it was first spoken to, and then seeing its parallel impact on our lives and situation. The crowd on the Day of Pentecost were left in no doubt about the relevance to them of what Peter was saying and preaching! His preaching required a verdict and he got it! (Acts 2:37–39).

There is an interesting comment by Sinclair Ferguson about what John Owen thought:

> It is of interest that Owen does not equate prophecy with preaching, simpliciter. Both may legitimately be regarded as forms of ministry of the Word, and consequently must be intimately related in form and content; nevertheless, there is a sense of immediacy about the idea of prophecy which is not necessarily present in the idea of preaching.[26]

It is my deeply held conviction that what is desperately needed in the church today is this kind of prophetic preaching. That is, preaching that is expositional, that teaches Holy Scripture, but does more than that, it 'preaches its teaching' as Dr Martin Lloyd-Jones used to say. That preaching must be done by a preacher who has met with God as he has laboured prayerfully over his exposition of Scripture. He has allowed Scripture to encourage and challenge him, and so he comes out of the study with a message from God, that he earnestly prays will be blessed by God as he preaches it. He is entirely

---

[26] Sinclair B. Ferguson, *John Owen on the Christian Life* (Edinburgh: Banner of Truth, 1987), 206.

Preaching must be done
by a preacher who has
met with God as he has
laboured prayerfully
over his exposition
of Scripture.

dependent on God for that blessing and longs that the message of the Bible ('God preaching' – J I Packer's famous definition of the Bible) will fulfil what God intends and change lives.

That sort of studious, sincere, and above all Spirit-dependent preaching is what I mean by 'prophetic preaching' and it does change lives! There is a power about it. That is a 'prophecy' which perfectly fulfils Paul's description that 'the one who prophesies speaks to people for their upbuilding and encouragement and consolation ... the one who prophesies builds up the church' (1 Corinthians 14:3–4). People leave church having met with God, not just having been intellectually informed (important as that is in its place).

Essentially (though not exclusively), prophecy today is the word of God preached with urgency and immediacy. It has a 'Thus says the Lord' about it, and its effect can often be seen in someone coming out of church who says 'God spoke to me tonight'; or 'tonight's message described me to a tee, who told you what I was feeling vicar?!' A rather better comment than 'nice sermon vicar!'

This opening of Scripture in the power of the Spirit that testifies to Christ and seeks to draw people to him is surely at the heart of all 'forth-telling' of God's Word. Though it does not cover all that prophecy means in the New Testament, it is surely central to its meaning. I have no trouble with allowing a 'prophecy' on an important occasion imparting to a local church some wisdom about a situation, or future event, or even about individual concerns (as we see in Acts 11:27ff; 20:23; 21:9–14), which are particular to that church and therefore not to be enscripturated. Indeed, every utterance must be tested by Holy Scripture.[27]

Let me give you an example of what I mean. When I was Vicar of St Peter's, Harold Wood, a church that happily emphasised expository preaching, we had a special weekend on giving. On the Sunday, a much-loved and respected lay preacher came to me during the singing of a hymn. He said: 'I have a picture of us and our giving that I can't get out of my mind. Our giving is like an iceberg, only a small part of it is showing, and we need to give a lot more!' I called my fellow elders and shared what he said with them and we agreed that it was a perfect picture of where the church was at, and we asked him to share it with the congregation after we had finished the hymns we were singing. This resonated with the congregation, as it was a helpful visual aid of the Scriptures we had

---

[27] See further in J. P. Baker, 'Prophecy in the New Testament', in D. R. W. Wood, *ed., New Bible Dictionary, 3rd ed.* (Leicester: IVP, 1996), 974: 'All may agree that there is no new revelation to be expected concerning God in Christ, the way of salvation, the principles of the Christian life, etc. But there appears to be no good reason why the living God, who both speaks and acts (in contrast to the dead idols), cannot use the gift of prophecy to give particular local guidance to a church, nation or individual, or to warn or encourage by way of prediction as well as reminders, in full accord with the written word of Scripture, by which all such utterances must be tested.'

been teaching, and was a real blessing. We did not talk up this experience, nor did we expect it to happen regularly, but in a healthy congregation, things like this can and do happen from time to time.

However, let us importantly remember that it is the preaching of the apostolic gospel, it is the testimony to God's saving grace, and our need of Christ, that is the thing that discloses to an unbeliever 'the secrets of his heart', and 'so falling on his face, he will worship God and declare that God is really among you' (1 Corinthians 14:24–25). 'The preaching of the Word of God (*If it is faithful*), is the Word of God' (2nd Helvetic Confession, emphasis added) and it saves, blesses and builds up the church. Healthy churches see this happening every week!

The one who preaches is to remember that he is called to preach the very oracles of God (1 Peter 4:11). It is a huge responsibility which requires the best from those who prophesy and preach in the sense that I have outlined. God's people need to pray as much for their preachers as preachers do for their people. May God restore this kind of prophetic preaching to our churches and may we be content with nothing less than biblical, applied pastoral preaching that makes us listen to what God is saying to us. It is not about eloquence, but faithfulness, integrity and the power of the Holy Spirit at work.

Let Calvin have the last word in this section. While complaining about bad preaching but encouraging people to be patient with preachers who are faithful and

The one who preaches is to remember that he is called to preach the very oracles of God.

trying hard but sometimes 'miss the mark', he warns: 'Since the abolition of prophecy means the destruction of the Church, let us allow heaven and earth to fall into disorder rather than that prophecy should cease'.[28] These are serious words, so let us pray and work for a wider restoration of proper biblical proclamation in the power of the Spirit to the glory of God and the blessing of his people, and let us practice what we preach and advocate!

Peter's method

I want to add here a few further words on Peter's method of preaching on the day of Pentecost.

Firstly, *he starts where people were at*. The people are amazed and perplexed by what they have seen and heard, and they are asking questions 'What does this mean? (2:12)'. They want answers to what they have experienced. For many people today, the events may not be as dramatic as they were on this occasion, but they still want answers to the questions of life and particularly answers that address the meaning of life as they are experiencing it.

Secondly, Peter wants them *to interpret the perplexities of life by understanding them in the light of what Scripture teaches*. He carefully expounds the three passages of Scripture so as to show their relevance to the people's questions and to give them satisfying answers. It is not all exhortation, but is full of carefully considered content, that provides the

---

[28] John Calvin, *1 Thessalonians* (Edinburgh: Saint Andrew Press, 1972), 378.

substance to call the people to repentance. It also shows the continuity between the Old Testament promises and the New Testament fulfilment of them.

Thirdly, *he tells the story of Jesus*, his life and how God did mighty works, wonders and signs through him (2:22). Peter speaks of his crucifixion as not some tragic end to an otherwise exemplary life but as the fulfilment of God's plan (2:23). He speaks about how God raised Jesus from the dead, as his vindication, as bearing in mind who he was and is, it was not possible for death to hold him. All the time he seeks to bear testimony to the Lord Jesus. Acts 2:36 is the key verse in his preaching: 'Let all the house of Israel therefore know for certain that God has made him both Lord and Christ, this Jesus whom you crucified.' Peter's preaching is Christ-centred and seeks not glory for the preacher but for the Lord!

Fourthly, *application is built in as he goes along and flows from the testimony of Scripture and the reality of the Easter events* (2:23, 33) – not just at the end. He is enabling God-given understanding to take place among his listeners, as he explains the gospel to them.

Fifthly, and importantly, it is the *power of the message and the work of the Spirit* that pressurises the crowd to ask 'Brothers, what shall we do?' (2:37). Only the Spirit can 'cut to the heart'. Peter has a clear answer to what they should do, and he exhorts them to experience the God-sent salvation made possible through the life, death and resurrection of the Lord Jesus. His preaching demands a response, a verdict – but it is not human pressure or techniques that bring the people to their knees. It is the gospel, 'the power of God for salvation to everyone who believes' (Rom 1:16) that is having its effect. Peter was leading and feeding the people responsibly and well, but he was not manipulating them one bit!

Preachers need to remember what they are called to do with all their might, but it is not our work to save – only God can do that – it is our job to explain the gospel, bear witness to the Lord Jesus, and proclaim the Saviour of the world. We should pray for, and long for, a God-given response, but not seek to 'make' it ourselves!

Conclusion

There is then a spectrum of prophecy from testimony to the special calling of a preacher. All this is of considerable importance to the life of the local church.

First, if Christians are a prophetic people called to display the spirit of prophecy by their testimony to Jesus, then more space ought to be given in congregational life for people to testify to what the Lord has done and is doing in their lives. Also, what encouragements, warnings and blessings they are being taught by the Holy Spirit from their reading and studying of the Holy Scriptures which he inspired. This of course needs monitoring by the church eldership and any excesses restrained.

Speaking personally, in our more informal evening service, which majors on teaching and preaching the

Word at a deeper level than is possible in the mornings, more space could and should be given, from time to time, to hear what God is doing in people's lives. This always has an impact on people, and enables the church to function more as a body with each appropriately making a contribution to congregational life. It also has a way of earthing good preaching, allowing people to say what they have found helpful in the teaching programme of the church. All this helps folk to grasp truth and be fired up by it.

I am also convinced that the more we share with one another in church life our testimonies to God's grace and goodness, the easier we will find it to bear witness in public to our friends and neighbours. This is important as there is so often considerable difficulty in getting Christians to take God-given opportunities to testify to Jesus, and learn to speak naturally to others about him. If we see that done in church, we learn how to do it better. All this assumes that if opportunities are given to speak in church, people are taught and encouraged to give the glory to Jesus and that it is not all about themselves!

When I was a young teenage Christian, my family and I attended a Plymouth Brethren Assembly (Open Brethren) for a while, until we moved back near an Anglican Evangelical congregation. On Sunday mornings, at the 'Breaking of Bread', there would be an opportunity for people to give a testimony or share a verse that had blessed them. Sometimes there was a queue, sometimes not. However, the most instructive and helpful ministry was given by senior Brethren men, mostly senior businessmen who in those bygone days had spare time during their afternoons at work! They would spend valuable time reading and studying the Bible with a view to sharing something on Sunday if appropriate. It was generally very good exposition, and there may have been two such messages (rarely more). All this seemed very spontaneous, and most of the testimonies seemed so, but the longer considered and most helpful messages came from prayerful men, saturated in Scripture, who spent time studying so that they could teach a congregation on Sunday. All this does not seem that different to what was happening in the Corinthian church as recorded in 1 Corinthians 14, except that perhaps then the work of the Spirit was more direct for a while until the church had the New Testament Scriptures available to them. Most wise and growing Brethren Assemblies today, when businessmen have less time to study the Bible, have appointed pastors/teachers to fulfil their role, as God intended in the first place! (see Ephesians 4:11ff).

Secondly, if all that I have been saying is true, then more ought to be done to improve the standard of preaching. This is often very poor in many churches. This will start with asking a congregation to pray regularly for their preaching team – that God will use them and speak through them. Too often in faithful and well taught churches I know of, the prayer time in home groups neglects to pray for the Sunday preaching. As the health of the church depends on the teaching and preaching of

God's Word, then priority time must be given and taken by the preachers to pray and prepare well for Sunday, and other preaching opportunities. In one large congregation I served, the senior minister was given three weeks' study leave a year (apart from holidays). This enabled me to get away with my family each half-term and prepare and work through sermon series. Not every church can do that, but preachers must not be expected to be omni-competent, but given time to prepare well.

We have seen what that meant in Peter's life as expressed by his preaching on the Day of Pentecost, without which the crowd would have remained in ignorance as to what God was doing among the disciples of Jesus, and could do for them. His preaching came from the recommissioning of the Lord to him to 'feed my sheep' (John 21). Peter knew what God had called him to do. There was also the period of prayer when individually and together the disciples waited for the fulfilment of the promise of the risen Lord to them to be fulfilled (Acts 1:8, 14). The background of Peter's ministry was prayer – it was a ministry bathed in prayer.

Furthermore, Peter, like the other disciples, would have been deeply thinking about what the risen Christ taught the disciples on the road to Emmaus (Luke 24), about all of Scripture bearing witness to him. They will have been pondering on Scripture, and also what Jesus had taught them, in the light of the Easter event. His substitutionary death for them and his triumph over death displayed by the resurrection changed everything!

All of Scripture, 'the whole counsel of God' as Paul puts it in Acts 20, must now be taught faithfully and in a way that bears witness to the living Lord, who had executed the Father's plan of redemption for his elect people from every nation on earth. This meant that Peter, and the others, must proclaim the promises of God revealed in the Old Testament as fulfilled by the life, death and resurrection of the Lord Jesus. In modern parlance, they needed to understand Biblical Theology – the progressive and cumulative revelation of God through the prophets of old, now completed in God revealing himself in his unique and beloved Son, and the apostolic witness to that (Hebrews 1:1–4). In our terms, they would start to preach the Bible, both Old and New Testaments, canonically and theologically as being all about Jesus!

With the help of the Holy Spirit that in turn would be applied to a congregation, requiring a response of repentance and faith. This in turn would make new disciples of the Lord Jesus. For he alone is the unique and only Saviour that the world has been given. This is what happened through Peter's preaching on the day of Pentecost!

How will this happen among us today? We are not Apostles, as Peter was, but our preaching ministry is analogous to his, as we proclaim the apostolic faith today. Following the model of Peter here, we can see the importance of the steps he took and the principles he practised, which should be paralleled in us preachers today:

- A sense of calling, with a message to proclaim

- Prayerfulness, a ministry dependent on God and bathed in prayer

- Deep meditation on Holy Scripture and the teaching of Jesus in the light of the Easter event

- Courageous exposition and proclamation of revealed truth, bearing witness to Jesus and enabled by the Holy Spirit

- A message requiring a response – which is not simply the imparting of information

- Through this kind of proclamation, new disciples of Jesus are made and the church grows!

It greatly concerns me that the first Christian sermon on the Day of Pentecost in Acts 2 has not become among us the paradigm and model of how to preach that it should be and that the Lord surely intended. I firmly believe that we need to think again about the place and power of this kind of prophetic expository preaching, which is central to the healthy life of a local congregation, as well as the calling and duty of the whole redeemed people of God to be a prophetic people bearing testimony to their Lord and Saviour Jesus Christ. These things grasped and practised in a fresh way would, I am convinced, make local churches far more effective in winning people for the Lord and building up to maturity believers who are growing and effective as witnesses for Christ.

Let us then, with fresh insight and courage, pray and seek for these things to be more and more true and taken to heart among us!

Wallace Benn
Pentecost 2022

Other recommendations

In our Christian Leadership series:

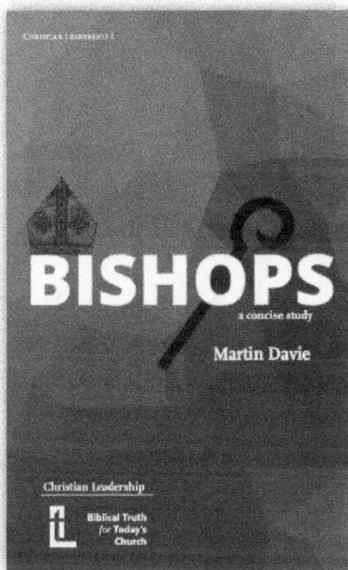

Bishops Past, Present and Future: A Concise Study summarises the key points of the argument of Martin's major study *Bishops Past, Present and Future* (Gilead Books 2022). It is designed to meet the needs of those who would like to know about the role and importance of bishops in the Church of England, but who would baulk at tackling the 800+ pages of the original book.

This concise study is published in the hope that it will help many in the Church of England, both ordained and lay, to think in a more informed fashion about how bishops should respond to the challenges facing the Church of England at this critical point in its history as it considers how to move forward following the publication of the Living in Love and Faith material.

Also published by the Latimer Trust:

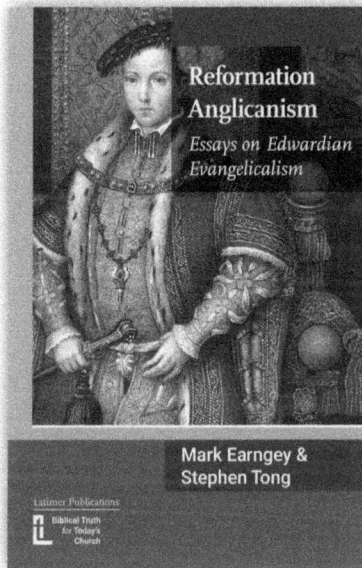

Reformation Anglicanism: Essays on Edwardian Evangelicalism is a superb set of essays arising from the Moore Theological College symposium on Reformation Anglicanism held in 2019. Featuring essays from various reformation scholars, this collection of articles focuses on some foundational documents (e.g. *Book of Homilies*, *Articles of Religion*) and foundational reformers (e.g. Thomas Cranmer, Martin Bucer, Heinrich Bullinger) involved with the English Reformation, and its Edwardian phase in particular. This edited volume not only offers a sustained focus on the often neglected mid-Tudor phase of the Reformation but explores new avenues of research on overlooked subjects such as the *45 Articles of Religion*, John Ponet's *Short Catechism*, the *Reformatio Legum Ecclesiasticarum*, the ministry of

John Hooper, and the memory of Martin Bucer. Students and scholars alike will benefit from this fresh examination of these anchors of Anglicanism which were hotly contested both then, and now.

Together in Love & Faith?

SHOULD THE CHURCH BLESS SAME-SEX PARTNERSHIPS?

A RESPONSE TO THE BISHOP OF OXFORD

VAUGHAN ROBERTS

Writing from his own experience of same-sex attraction, Vaughan Roberts responds to the Bishop of Oxford's argument that the Church of England should change its doctrine and practice in relation to same-sex relationships. He outlines the beauty and goodness of the Bible's teaching on sex and marriage, as traditionally understood, and calls for it to be upheld with sensitivity and pastoral wisdom.

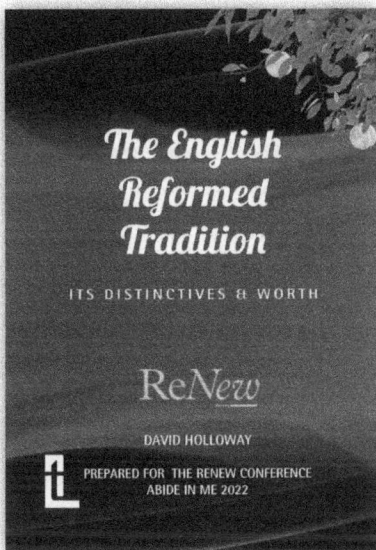

The English Reformed Tradition

ITS DISTINCTIVES & WORTH

ReNew

DAVID HOLLOWAY

PREPARED FOR THE RENEW CONFERENCE
ABIDE IN ME 2022

The Reformation in Europe produced different traditions according to the influential people and theological climate of each country. But what is it that makes the English Reformed tradition as expressed in the Church of England? This short booklet, produced for Renew, considers the Anglican distinctives as compared with other Reformed traditions, and the enduring importance of preserving this rich heritage.

www.ingramcontent.com/pod-product-compliance
Lightning Source LLC
Chambersburg PA
CBHW020437030426
42337CB00014B/1295